NURSING'S VISION *for* PRIMARY HEALTH CARE

in the 21 *st* CENTURY

LUCY N. MARION
PH.D., R.N., C.S.

AMERICAN NURSES ASSOCIATION

Library of Congress Cataloging-in-Publication Data

Marion, Lucy N.
   Nursing's vision for primary health care in the 21st century / by Lucy N. Marion.
      p. cm.
   Includes bibliographical references.
   ISBN 1-55810-124-1
   1. Nursing—United States—Forecasting. 2. Primary health care—United States. 3.
Twenty-first
century—Forecasts. I. American Nurses Association. II. Title.
   [DNLM: 1. Nursing—trends—United States. 2. Primary Health Care—trends—United
States.
WY 16 M341n 1996]
RT4.M345 1996
610.73′0973—dc20
DNLM/DLC
for Library of Congress

96-10795
CIP

Published by
American Nurses Publishing
600 Maryland Ave., SW
Suite 100 West
Washington, DC 20024

ACKNOWLEDGMENTS

The Congress of Nursing Practice wishes to acknowledge and thank Jean E. Steele, Ph.D., R.N., for the early ground-breaking work that serves as the foundation for this paper.

Congress of Nursing Practice, 1994–1996

Mary K. Walker, Ph.D., R.N., F.A.A.N., Chairperson
Katreena R. Collette, M.S., R.N.
Jo A. Franklin, M.S., R.N., C.N.A.
Judith E. Haber, Ph.D., R.N., C.S., F.A.A.N.
Gail A. Harkness, Dr.P.H., R.N., F.A.A.N.
Mary S. Koithan, Ph.D., R.N.
Fang-lan Wang Kuo, Ed.D., R.N.
Frank P. Lamendola, M.S.N., R.N., C.S.
Tona L. Leiker, M.N., A.R.N.P., C.A.R.N.
Karen S. Martin, M.S.N., R.N., F.A.A.N.
Judith L. Martin-Holland, M.S., M.P.A., R.N.
Kathleen M. Poi, M.S., R.N., C.N.A.A.
Maureen E. Shekleton, D.N.Sc., R.N.
Susan Tullai-McGuinness, M.P.A., R.N.
Julie M. Wooden, R.N.,C., C.C.R.N.

Reviewers

Rosemary Camilleri, Ph.D.
Claire Fagin, Ph.D., R.N., F.A.A.N.
Joyce Fitzpatrick, Ph.D., R.N., F.A.A.N.
Marie Lindsey, M.S., R.N., C.S.
Judith McDevitt, M.S., R.N., C.S.
Terry Misener, Ph.D., R.N., C.S., F.A.A.N.
Juliann Sebastian, Ph.D., R.N.
Diana Taylor, Ph.D., R.N., C.S., F.A.A.N.
Judith Thompson

ANA Staff

Rita Munley Gallagher, Ph.D., R.N.,C.

TABLE OF CONTENTS

FOREWORD

by Joyce J. Fitzpatrick, Ph.D., R.N., F.A.A.N.

Health care today reflects one of the most rapidly changing environments. There are changes in expectations among consumers, purchasers, and providers. And, most important, there is a search for increased quality, that is, excellence in care delivery, at a reduced cost. Questions about provider productivity and intervention effectiveness linger. The search for a new view and a reorganization of the system of care delivery continues to influence public policy and affect private investments and decisions.

Thus, as the twenty-first century approaches, the United States faces one of its most challenging internal issues: how to reorient a health care system that is overpriced yet delivers excellent health care to those Americans with access to the system and its providers. In a nation abundant with resources, we have led the world in many dimensions of health care. Biomedical research and high-technology interventions in medical care delivery in the United States are acclaimed throughout the world. More recently, however, our attention has been redirected to a new view of the health care landscape, that of primary care, including all aspects of care delivery focused on comprehensive, coordinated care. As a nation, we are struggling to reorient ourselves and our system to care that is longitudinal rather than episodic; comprehensive rather than specific; community- and patient-directed rather than provider-driven; and population-based rather than individualistic.

Nurses are well-positioned for leadership roles in this changing and challenging health care system. A time-honored philosophical base will guide nursing throughout these and future changes. As reflected in our roots as public health nurses, community health activists, and patient advocates, professional nurses long have understood the issues related to community-based care and patient involvement in choices about treatment and care delivery. While an important part of the history of professional nursing development, collaborative practice among health professionals also will be an increased necessity in the restructured health care delivery systems. No longer can we afford individualized practices and independent decision-making. Collaboration among health professionals represents our best efforts to effect change toward the goal of enhanced health care for U.S. citizens.

This document, nursing's view of primary care, reflects the state of the art of both intra-disciplinary and interdisciplinary practice. Issues of relevance to future delivery designs are captured and framed within the primary care context. This work represents the most current assessment of the primary care dimensions of discipline-specific nursing issues, and broader health care concerns of interest to nursing.

The American Nurses Association is to be commended for supporting this work and bringing the core issues of the future of health care delivery to the forefront of public discussion. This manuscript represents a slice in time, as the 1995 description of primary care, and charts the course for future generations of providers and recipients of care.

EXECUTIVE SUMMARY

Over a century ago, the legendary public health nurse Lillian Wald cared for New York's poor in the Henry Street Settlement (Wald 1934). Since then, nurses have delivered general, personal health care to individuals, families, and communities. In the late 1950s and 1960s, nurses advanced their practices with baccalaureate and graduate education, research, and innovative roles. Nurses increasingly became responsible for support of client self care, education and counseling, referrals and follow-up, and preventive measures in public health, primary care, and acute care. Advanced practice nurses (APNs), prepared at the graduate level, now provide a full range of primary care services and are accountable for their clients' outcomes. Collaborating with other clinicians throughout the health care delivery system, primary care nurses are unique with their expertise in integrating low-tech interventions, attention to psychosocial issues, client self-care approaches, and coordinated care management.

Presently, the health care system is challenged by high costs, overspecialization, marked inequities among populations, and fragmentation of care. Corporate America and state and federal governments are responding to economic problems with rapid and dramatic cost-containment measures. Within this context, nursing offers a caring, humanistic yet ecological, and practical vision for health care in the twenty-first century. First, all people will have access to essential health services. Also, the health care system will reflect the World Health Organization's concept of primary health care— an approach in which individuals, professionals, and community groups form partnerships to address health problems they view as priority (WHO 1978).

Finally, APNs and other nurses envision a system in which they can practice to the full extent of their abilities in caring for all people, especially vulnerable populations.

Nurses believe that a quality, cost-effective health care system requires a solid primary care foundation. Primary care is the accessible, prevention-oriented, general wellness and illness care of individuals and families. Primary care includes health assessment, health promotion, and health maintenance; diagnosis and management of common acute and chronic illnesses; and support of a dignified and comfortable death. Primary care is continuing, comprehensive, and coordinated, beginning with first-contact care. Primary care is holistic, client-centered, caring, and knowledge-based. The client and clinician have a mutually respectful relationship and share responsibility for health care and health outcomes. The primary care clinician coordinates specialty health services. Ideally primary care clinician teams are interdisciplinary, with shared decision-making authority, shared goals, and partnerships with clients.

Nursing's vision for a new health care system includes comprehensive integrated delivery systems founded on decentralized primary care networks and a revitalization of the U.S. public health system. Comprehensive integrated delivery systems will assure ready access to hospitals, long-term and subacute care facilities, home care, and other services. When essential health care is accessible to all, the public health system will focus on health policy, health promotion, and disease prevention; conduct research and health surveillance; and form partnerships with private organizations to share health care expertise.

Baccalaureate and graduate nursing education prepares nurses for roles within the new integrated delivery systems. These nurses now deliver more primary care, perform more independently, and manage client care more efficiently than ever before. The graduate programs will need additional funding strategies to meet new demands for advanced practice nurses. Furthermore, unwarranted barriers to advanced practice nurses and other qualified clinicians must be removed. With recent changes in nursing curricula, sufficient funding, and removal of practice barriers, nurses will continue to increase their contributions to the delivery and administration of primary care.

Recommendations

The nursing vision for primary care in the twenty-first century has requisite objectives and strategies. The following recommendations reflect necessary changes if the nation's health care system is to meet its potential to provide quality, cost-effective health care.

Recommendation 1

Establish primary care principles as the foundation of professional practice for all providers.
- Provide holistic, client-centered, and appropriate health care for all.
- Emphasize health promotion, disease prevention, early intervention, and client self care.
- Coordinate secondary and tertiary care from the primary care base.
- Balance current health care knowledge with client wishes and characteristics in managing health problems.
- Assure accessible care by removing cost, communication, and transportation obstacles, and other barriers.

Recommendation 2

Provide for an adequate workforce of primary care providers.
- Increase educational support for primary care, multicultural, and community-based training of health professionals.
- Establish new funding to support graduate primary care nursing education.
- Support collaborative interdisciplinary primary care training programs.
- Remove practice barriers for APNs and other qualified primary care providers.

Recommendation 3

Establish a method of primary care delivery for all people.
- Provide health care coverage that includes primary care and preventive services, starting with those at the beginning of life and then other vulnerable uninsured populations.
- Develop multiple strategies utilizing public/private partnerships to finance health care coverage.
- Restructure health care financing to reward primary and preventive care.

Recommendation 4

Develop public and private partnerships to create a new structure for health care delivery.

- Build a new system with primary care as the broad and stable base.
- Develop a dense, decentralized, community-oriented primary care delivery network with numerous sites where people live and work.
- Create integrated delivery systems that provide comprehensive. co-ordinated services.
- Revitalize the U.S. public health system to address public health promotion and disease prevention policies; conduct research and health surveillance; and form public/private partnerships to deliver health care and share technical expertise.
- Develop multiple strategies utilizing public/private partnerships to finance health care for all people.

INTRODUCTION

This monograph presents nursing's vision for primary care in the twenty-first century. This vision has evolved from more than 100 years of planning and delivering health care by nurses within the context of changing sociocultural, economic, and political forces. Based on the realities of the past and present and the expectations of the future, nursing describes its role in health care and recommends strategies to improve the nation's health, via primary care. The principles set forth in this document will help to guide the nursing profession as it enters the next century.

During the twentieth century, health care in the United States evolved from a low-tech, humanistic, community-based service to a high-tech specialty industry. General physicians and nurses, compassionate health advisors to the family, were replaced by teams of specialists focused on treating and/or curing disease. These and other trends related to health care resulted in estimated costs of more than one trillion dollars, or more than 15 percent, of the gross domestic product in 1995 (Burner, Waldo, and McKusick 1992).

The challenges of reframing the U.S. health care system have driven the search for innovation. Federal and state legislation has begun to open the field of primary care to a variety of health providers in response to the demand for fundamental change. Business and governments have implemented managed care, usually as an attractive cost-saving option to indemnity plans. Prevention, a logical approach to cost-containment, is an integral part of managed care. States are experimenting with a variety of insurance reforms, and legislators recognize a need for malpractice reform. Also, U.S. health care planners are monitoring other national models of health care delivery.

Primary Care: Pathway to the Nation's Health

Primary care emerged in the 1960s as the contemporary method of personal health care (Fagin 1993; Lewy 1977). Private health insurance, Medicare and Medicaid, and the general consumer rights movements helped to spawn a health care rights drive. The public called for professional management not only of illness, but also for preventive and wellness care. New primary care systems were developed. Researchers developed a body of knowledge related to primary care and its outcomes, delivery systems, and evaluation (Starfield 1992). The success of primary care is measured in terms of preventing disease as well as halting the progression of disease and disability. Also, client satisfaction with the health care process and resulting quality of life are important outcomes.

As the United States has redirected its attention to cost-effective health care, primary care has assumed greater importance. Currently, primary care is not equitably distributed to the nation's vulnerable populations; distribution is inadequate in rural and some urban areas. All other Western industrialized nations have well-developed systems of primary care, and their citizens have better health outcomes in terms of life expectancy and infant mortality than citizens in the United States. (Schieber, Poullier, and Greenwald 1994).

Several groups and authors have proposed definitions of primary care (Starfield 1992; IOM 1978, 1984; AAN 1976; Alpert and Charney 1973; Millis 1966;). The definitions represent a conceptual evolution that encompasses health care provided by various clinicians; the activities in which they engage; the level of care or the settings in which they practice; contextual attributes; and, the strategies upon which the health care system as a whole is arranged. Most recently, the interdisciplinary Committee on the Future of Primary Care of the Institute of Medicine (IOM) proposed the following definition in its Interim Report:

> Primary care is the provision of integrated, accessible health care services by clinicians who are accountable for addressing a large majority of personal health care needs, developing sustained partnership with patients, and practicing in the context of family and community (IOM 1994, p. 1).

The nursing perspective on primary care is essentially compatible with the IOM Interim Report. Nurses define primary care as prevention-oriented general wellness and illness care for individuals and families. The recipients of care are often called "clients," representing the contractual and assistive nature of the client-clinician relationship. Primary care is continuing and comprehensive: it includes first-contact care; health assessment, health promotion, and health maintenance; and diagnosis and management of common acute and chronic illnesses; and it supports a dignified and comfortable death. Nurses believe that primary care is holistic, client-centered, caring, and appropriate for the person, family, and community. The client and clinician have a continuing and mutually respectful relationship.

To be effective, primary care must be accessible—without barriers related to cost, availability, communication, or location. A full range of health services are coordinated to avoid costly gaps and overlaps. Contemporary primary care teams consist of members from different disciplines who together meet a greater variety of clients' health needs. The team members practice in a collegial and collaborative manner. While primary care clinicians provide care mostly in ambulatory settings, they also care for clients in their homes, acute and long-term care institutions, and residential settings. Interdisciplinary team practice includes: collaborative decision-making, open communication among team members, awareness of the complementary skills of team members, and a focus on patient participation and health outcomes.

Nurses believe that primary care systems should reflect the principles of primary health care: collaboration among individuals, community, and professionals to determine what health problems to address and how; every individual's right to essential health care and responsibility for self care and for supporting the community's health; and emphasis on health promotion and prevention of health problems rather than cure of illness (WHO 1978). Development of health systems is integrated within the overall social and economic development. Primary health care is oriented to a community and its culture(s). Primary care, as a vital subset of primary health care, is personal health care for individuals and families (Barnes et al. 1995; McElmurry 1994).

Primary Care: Foundation of the Health Care System

In an efficient health care system, primary care is the largest part of the total system. Health care can be envisioned with three interdependent segments: primary, secondary, and tertiary care. These segments once represented a type of setting and type of clinician, e.g., with tertiary care, the cardiovascular surgeon working in surgery and the coronary care unit. However, the advent of comprehensive, coordinated systems has blurred the roles and boundaries. Clinicians deliver their services in a variety of settings, focusing on client need rather than the environment in which care is rendered.

Primary care forms the broad and deep base of the health care system by providing initial and continuing care and appropriate access to the other types of care. Primary care clinicians offer entry, continuing, and comprehensive care to individuals and families. While these clinicians use low levels of technology, they use high levels of assessment and interpersonal skills. The primary care clinician serves as a client advocate and coordinates secondary and tertiary services through referral and collaboration. Primary care nurses are advanced practice nurses (APNs), including family, pediatric, women's health, adult, and gerontological nurse practitioners (NPs), certified nurse-midwives (CNMs), selected clinical nurse specialists (CNSs), and nurses prepared in community/public health care in baccalaureate nursing programs. In an integrated system, primary care is woven throughout ambulatory sites, clients' homes, and residential settings, such as nursing homes and prisons.

Secondary care is disease-specific care, often requiring the expertise of a health care specialist to diagnose and treat the problem. However, the primary care clinician may continue to direct the care in these settings. The focus is to reverse or arrest disease and prevent disability. Nurses in secondary care include CNSs (e.g., oncology and psychiatric/mental health), primary and acute care nurse practitioners, care/case managers, nurse anesthetists, and nurses with basic preparation. Nurses may be responsible for care management during prolonged illness and disability, thus integrating primary and long-term care. Physicians include general surgeons and specialists in all fields of medicine and their physician assistants. Secondary care settings include specialty clinics, private practices, hospitals, and nursing homes. When possible, secondary care is provided until the client's problem is stabilized, and the client is returned to the primary care provider.

Tertiary care is emergent and critical care, the smallest component of the health care system. Nurses include CNSs, nurse anesthetists, acute care nurse practitioners who merge the CNS and NP roles (Keane and Richmond 1993), and staff nurses who provide most of the client's direct care. Physicians include subspecialists in all fields of medicine and surgery. The clinicians are highly trained specialists who utilize technological interventions in intensive care, coronary care, and trauma centers. The focus is on preventing death and disability. When the client recovers from a critical illness or enters the terminal phase, the primary care clinician increases or resumes full care.

A Client-Centered Approach

Primary care is client-centered, taking into account the background, needs, and strengths of the whole person and/or the family. Holistic assessment of mental and physical health takes place within the context of the client's age, gender, race, socioeconomic and cultural status, environment, family, and community. Family care includes assessment and management of the family unit in meeting health needs, e.g., a family coping with a member's mental illness or lead poisoning of its children. The clinician interacts with the client in a caring manner, demonstrating the willingness and ability to listen, to hear what is said, and to respond with empathy. The clinician protects the client's right to informed choice and control over health care decisions. Together, the client and clinician select procedures and treatments after discussing potential benefits and negative outcomes and costs.

Primary care is comprehensive, spanning the health continuum. It includes promoting health; preventing disease; treating illness, preferably at early stages; and providing for a dignified death (ANA 1987). When appropriate services are beyond the primary care clinician's scope of practice, the clinician refers the clients to specialists, taking care to evaluate specialty services in terms of client satisfaction, cost, and health outcomes.

An efficient primary care system designs entry care, an initial step of coordinated and continuing care to eliminate costly gaps and overlaps. During entry, the client meets a primary care clinician and/or a team of clinicians. The client is oriented to the setting and services. From a complete health history and physical examination, the client and clinician identify health and illness needs. The clinician addresses acute or non-acute health care needs within the first encounter and schedules additional appointments as necessary. Some urgent preventive needs, such as childhood immunizations and adolescent contraception information and services, are managed immediately. Entry care includes prompt referral for complex medical and surgical problems (ANA 1985; 1987).

Continuing care occurs first through timely appointments with a primary care clinician. Acute and/or new conditions are treated and return appointments are scheduled for follow-up care. Urgent care may be provided on a walk-in basis. When possible, the client sees the same primary care clinician or team to maintain continuity of services. Continuity of care provides the stable, caring base necessary for a therapeutic relationship and promotes mutual client-provider understanding and appreciation (ANA 1987). When the client-provider relationship is not positive, the client should be able to choose another clinician whenever possible.

Coordinated care may include the simple follow-up of a referral to a specialist, a postcard or home visit to a family whose child is not immunized, and full care/case management of a client disabled from a work-related injury. In managed care, coordination also includes the process of gatekeeping, which is a mandated and controlled method of referral to specialists while maintaining the primary care clinician role and resuming client care as soon as possible. Furthermore, the primary care clinician gives care and/or maintains contact as the client moves from setting to setting, such as nursing homes and hospitals. Coordination also implies prompt entry and efficient retrieval of health data, reducing the waste of repetitious history-taking, physical examination, and various tests.

Coordination of care (care/case management) is a standard professional nursing function that has further evolved within comprehensive integrated multi-service health systems. The success of APNs' care of clients with clinical mental illness (Moller 1994), medical fragility (Trella 1993), and preventive needs has been well-documented (Erkel 1993). APN coordination of the care of selected vulnerable clients in comprehensive integrated managed-care organizations has reduced drastically the need for neonatal intensive care (Alverson 1994) and the hospitalization of clients with arthritis (Anderson 1994). As coordination and case management interface with or expand to more primary care sites, costs should decrease while health care outcomes should continue to improve.

An overriding goal of primary care is to prevent disease, disability, and/or death in balance with the client's desired quality of life. Preventive care has been overlooked too often in our disease-oriented health care system (Davis et al. 1990). Prevention lacks glamour: there are no "problems" to solve, no symptoms to remove, and no dramatic cures. There are significant cost savings, though, with many prevention methods. And, while prevention is not always less expensive than a cure in cost-benefit analyses (Tengs et al. 1994; Russell 1992), quality of life cannot be quantified for the individual. More research is needed to determine the types, costs, and outcomes of preventive care that helps clients to preserve health and prevent health problems.

Health promotion and disease prevention interventions maintain or enhance health. Health promotion can include a provider's simple advice, which has been shown to change health behaviors in some clients. An office environment portraying the value of healthful behaviors may change others (USPHS 1994; Dickey 1993). The primary care clinician recommends good nutrition, exercise, stress reduction, and adequate rest, as well as supportive social networks and self-help groups. Each age and stage of development, including childhood, pregnancy, and aging, have specific health promotion needs. For example, disease prevention via childhood immunizations is a priority in primary care. Immunizations are administered at every possible opportunity: during well child visits, sick child visits within guidelines, and at sites away from the medical office, including schools.

Early detection can prevent progression of disease in asymptomatic clients (Davis 1993). Early detection traditionally has been limited to procedures such as blood pressure screening or laboratory tests to identify risk factors or the presence of disease. However, early detection increasingly applies to the identification of client risk factors and counseling to reduce risk through behavioral change, such as smoking cessation, stress management, and weight reduction.

The Office of Disease Prevention and Health Promotion of the U.S. Public Health Service has developed screening and preventive interventions and recommended preventive health guidelines for more than 60 major causes of disease and death. These guidelines are based on an appraisal of scientific evidence and clinical judgments of effectiveness in reducing the severity and incidence of disease. Widescale implementation of these guidelines should improve Americans' health (Davis et al. 1990). Put Prevention into Practice (PPIP) is a major national public health initiative to educate clinicians about research findings leading to preventive protocols (Griffith 1994). PPIP materials include the Clinician's Handbook of Preventive Services (USPHS 1994) to guide clinician decision-making. PPIP also has prevention flow sheets, stickers for client records to alert providers of special prevention needs, handout materials, and wall posters. To assist clients with health maintenance (Dickey 1993), PPIP designed a "mini record" personal health guide that informs, gives risk factors, and provides a record of preventive services.

Illness care also has a preventive goal to obviate disruption in life, to stop or reverse disease when possible, and to prevent disability and untimely death. In secondary and tertiary care settings, primary care clinicians collaborate with and refer to other clinicians. When clients recover from severe illnesses and injuries, they may need rehabilitative services. The goal is to maximize the individual's residual functional status. The primary care clinician coordinates rehabilitation while meeting other primary care needs.

Support of a comfortable and dignified death includes prevention of pain, loneliness, and loss of control to make decisions about one's remaining life and impending death. This goal demands that client and family preferences be understood, and necessary community resources be available. The primary care clinician determines the wishes of the client from advance directives and advocates for these wishes. When specialty care can no longer provide hope for cure or improvement in the quality of a person's remaining life, the primary care clinician resumes care of the client. Hospice and other home care nurses provide services to the client and family. The primary care clinician provides care to the family during and after the loss of a family member.

Prevention Saves Money and Lives

- Nine modifiable factors that often result in chronic conditions (smoking, diet/activity, alcohol, microbial agents, toxic agents, firearms, sexual behavior, motor vehicles, and illicit use of drugs) are major contributors to more than half of all deaths in the United States each year. Therefore, much of our national health expenditure is used for preventable diseases and injuries that are premature or are responsible for loss of potential years of life (McGinnis and Foege 1993).
- Every dollar spent on comprehensive prenatal care saves an average of $3 (U.S. Senate 1990, 101-417). Newborn and long-term health care costs for every low birthweight baby are reported to total between $14,000 and $30,525 and these costs are attributed largely to lack of prenatal care (OTA 1986). Prenatal care, even with the additional cost of a $100 financial incentive to the pregnant woman, had a zero dollar "cost per year of life saved" (Tengs et al. 1994, pp. 4,48).

- Over the last two decades, there has been a 40 percent drop in deaths due to heart disease. This marked decline reflects a dramatic rise in prevention methods. Providers monitor and control blood pressure, increase preventive screening of blood cholesterol levels, and educate consumers about risks of cigarette smoking and high-fat diets (USPHS 1990).

- Women age 65 and older are at high risk for cervical cancer. Yet of 15 million older women with incomes below the poverty level, 91 percent did NOT have a Pap test in 1992. The test costs $17—$24, whereas the total treatment cost for a single case of invasive cervical cancer is $28,000 (USPHS 1990). Cervical cancer screening every three years for women age 65 + had a zero dollar "cost per year of life saved" (Tengs et al. 1994, pp. 4, 43).

- Annual health care costs are 10 percent lower for children receiving primary care through Early Periodic Screening, Diagnosis and Treatment (EPSDT) Medicaid services (Children's Defense Fund 1990). EPSDT services include the physical exam; health, developmental, and nutritional assessment; screening for sensory, language, and blood abnormalities; and dental care.

- The economic cost of drug problems in 1990 was estimated to be $44 billion. The cost of attendant problems such as unwanted pregnancy, delinquency, and school failure was estimated to be $70 billion (USPHS 1990). According to the Harvard Center for Risk Analysis, all drug and alcohol treatments assessed for cost- effectiveness had a zero dollar "cost per year of life saved" (Tengs et al. 1994, pp. 4, 17, 44).

- The 1989–91 measles epidemic brought more than 55,467 cases and 132 related deaths, 11,251 hospitalizations for more than 44,100 hospital days, and costs estimated at $150 million. One year later, immunization services increased and parents became more aware as a result of public health promotion. The incidence of measles was slashed to 34 percent of the previous year, with 9,488 cases and approximately 30 deaths (Robinson et al. 1993). Like alcohol and drug treatment, childhood immunizations had a zero dollar "cost per year of life saved" (Tengs et al. 1994, pp. 4, 43).

A goal of primary care is to provide services appropriate not only for the client's needs but also for the family and community. From a health system's perspective, the appropriate primary care clinician is the competent, cost-containing, low-tech, prevention-oriented generalist. From the client's perspective, the appropriate clinician must be competent but also personally acceptable—perhaps having a similar cultural or racial background, being male or female, having a particular interactional style, or being attentive to time factors. For example, women of many cultures are uncomfortable with male clinicians performing pap smears and breast examinations. To accommodate the great diversity within the United States, clinicians must be culturally competent caregivers. The primary care facility should allow the client a choice of available clinicians.

Appropriate care includes the use of current knowledge for diagnosis and treatment of illness. All health care clinicians are held accountable for the way they treat illnesses (Pew 1993). By actuarial and other methods, auditors review the length of the visit, the diagnostic procedures, the type of medication, number of follow-up visits, the health outcome, client satisfaction, and the array of costs. Yet the primary care clinician must balance the art and science of health care to assure that care is responsive to the client as a person and appropriate to the health problem. Various groups, including the Agency for Health Care Policy and Research have developed guidelines for several common primary care problems (Sox and Woolf 1993). The clinician adjusts the guidelines to the individual client's needs, while being attentive to quality-of-life issues.

The effective health care system has accessible primary care, i.e., the system minimizes barriers related to cost, communication, location, and timing. These barriers are inextricably bound. For example, some minority groups have difficulty with the English language, their incomes are too low to pay health care bills or secure transportation, and they cannot afford to miss work for long waits in clinics. Each barrier must be addressed in the context of the others.

Cost barriers to primary care are widespread in the present system. Affordability of essential health care services varies with income, insurance, illnesses, number of family members, and other financial burdens. The poor need free or very low-cost care. People with catastrophic illnesses, temporarily unemployed people and their families, and other special groups periodically require free care. Insurance deductibles and co-payments can be cost barriers to many insured individuals and families. Some people cannot afford to lose hourly wages for a clinician visit; others cannot buy medications after paying the clinician's fee. Most providers, except emergency departments and charitable organizations, will not care for those who cannot pay. The general public incurs the high health care costs for progressive and irreversible illness and disabilities of the uninsured because of their lack of access to care in the early phases of illness.

The goal of essential health care for all people can be achieved only if services are affordable to the nation. To help assure affordable care, clinicians and clients must contain the growth of health care costs. Clients need education for self-care practices. Clinicians need to have a preventive orientation in routine practice. For example, a client health assessment upon entry to the system will identify and address health concerns early, before problems progress. Another strategy is to offer a full range of primary and secondary prevention services, such as family planning, dental care, and eye care, as well as a wellness plan for persons of all ages based on current guidelines (USPHS 1994). All health care consumers, except for the destitute, should share responsibility for health care by paying part of the bill. Tax-exempt health care organizations should contribute to the care of uninsured, low-income people. Finally, all people should contribute to containing costs by managing their own wellness and illness needs when they can.

Communication barriers exist when the client cannot explain what is wrong or worrisome, cannot understand the plan of care, or cannot interact to develop a working relationship with the clinician. Cultural and language differences can interfere with communication and lead to misunderstandings and ineffective client teaching and counseling. Clients with hearing and visual loss, mental illness, and intellectual deficits, as well as the very young and old have communicative needs. Using family members as translators, while helpful, removes confidentiality. Therefore, primary care clinicians should use language and teaching modalities that the client can understand or use neutral translators to assist with interactions. Teaching materials should be translated into the languages and the reading level of the clientele. Clinicians who generally are competent culturally often can overcome communication barriers, but feedback from the client is necessary to assure understanding.

Barriers related to availability decrease access to care. Lack of public services such as transportation affects the young, people with disabilities, and the elderly in particular. Health care access is often further limited by scarce and poorly placed health care sites, competing life demands such as work and care of family members, and little knowledge or understanding of the health care system. Fixed hours for clinic/office operation also reduce the availability of care; however, extended hours may not be useful if the location or transportation to and from the clinic are not safe. Therefore, clinic hours must reflect the best times for a particular clientele. In sparsely settled areas, home visits, mobile clinics, and clinics with traveling clinicians may improve access to care. "Telenursing" or "telepractice," the use of the telephone, fax, and the Internet, is evolving to become a major way to communicate with clients as they care for themselves at home.

Primary care must be available in a timely manner. Reducing waiting periods is a major strategy for improving clients' perceptions of provider care. In the true spirit of primary care, entry into the system should be unencumbered, offering walk-in, appointment, and telephone availability of professionals. These systems require constant monitoring to prevent gaps in necessary services. A staff that is committed to client satisfaction and efficient organization can reduce waiting times. A sufficient number and appropriate mix of clinicians are essential for maintaining client flow through the system. Finally, use of technology to register clients into the system and to track service and billing data contributes significantly to timeliness of care.

To increase availability of preventive services, primary care must integrate therapeutic regimens for episodes of acute and chronic conditions with continuing preventive care. The primary care clinician or a small team of clinicians should deliver the widest possible range of preventive care at initial and subsequent primary care visits along with the necessary client education to maximize the effects of their therapeutic interventions. Delays in providing immunizations, tuberculosis screening, sexually transmitted disease diagnosis and treatment, and contraceptive care compromise the client. With transient populations and other at-risk clients, the clinician should make every effort to detect and treat disease early in its course and to administer preventive measures each time the client is seen.

Summary

Primary care is the foundation of an effective health care delivery system and must become the pathway to the nation's health. Primary care is client-centered and, therefore, reflects a balance of current scientific knowledge with client characteristics and wishes. The success of primary care is measured in terms of preventing disease and halting the progression of disease and disability. Also, client satisfaction with the health care process and resulting quality of life is an important outcome. A health care system that is accessible and without barriers reinforces the success of existing services. Finally, low-tech, general primary care is a cost-effective alternative to the present specialty-oriented, high-tech system. For quality, cost-effective

Nurses as Primary Care Clinicians

For at least a century, nurses have delivered personal health care to sick and at-risk individuals and families as well as those with disabilities in community and public health settings. Lillian Wald provided health care to the poor in the Henry Street Settlement beginning in the 1890s (Coss 1992). As early as the 1920s and continuing today, the Frontier Nursing Service has employed family health nurses and nurse-midwives to serve families in remote areas (ACNM 1992). For decades, public health nurses have used protocols and medical consultation to provide health services for persons with sexually transmitted diseases and tuberculosis as well as child health, prenatal care, family planning, and other public health concerns (Crandall 1993). Community mental health nurses have cared for clients with acute and chronic mental illnesses in community and traditional public health settings (Krauss 1993).

The technological explosion in health care after World War II resulted in a dearth of generalist health care professionals (Fagin 1993; Lewy 1977). In response, nurses blended traditional acute care and community/public health nursing roles and skills, at first working with disadvantaged populations (DeAngelis 1994; Salmon 1993). Nurses also assumed responsibility for client counseling; continuity of care, including referrals and follow-up; prevention and self-care education; and encouraging the client to adhere to health advice. Further, medicine established the family practice "specialty" with standards, residency and continuing education requirements, and its own body of research-based knowledge (Lewy 1977). Specialists in medicine and surgery responded to the primary care demand by incorporating components of general health care into their specialties. Nurses, physicians, and others created interdisciplinary primary care teams.

The first nurse practitioner (NP) educational program was initiated in 1965 by Loretta Ford, Ed.D., R.N., and Henry Silver, MD (McGivern 1993; Wells 1993). NP masters programs soon followed. With advanced but generalist education, NPs formed the first advanced practice nursing (APN) "specialty" in which the nurse was accountable for a wide range of primary care services and client outcomes (DeAngelis 1994). Nurse practitioner practice and other types of advanced nursing practice gained momentum in the 1960s and 1970s and contributed to the APN model of primary care delivery. For example, psychiatric clinical nurse specialists maintained successful private practices, gained reimbursement, and advanced supportive health care legislation. Nurse practitioners now deliver comprehensive primary care to under/unserved individuals and families, and other APNs contribute a variety of services that interface with primary care within health care delivery systems.

Clinician Supply: Nurses and Physicians

Primary care is poorly distributed in the United States, creating a shortage mostly for vulnerable populations. If the approximately sixty million under/uninsured Americans did receive primary care, demand could increase by 15 percent (Council on Graduate Medical Education 1992). Much of the maldistribution is due to the lack of available primary care clinicians, mostly nurses and physicians. This is particularly true in inner city and rural areas of the nation. Nurses who deliver primary care include advanced practice nurses, such as NPs, certified nurse midwives (CNMs), and selected clinical nurse specialists (CNSs). Additionally, nurses prepared at the basic level perform many primary care functions (OTA 1986). The traditional primary care physician is certified in family medicine or is prepared at the general practitioner level. Many medical and surgical specialty physicians, such as gynecologists, internists, and pediatricians, provide some primary care services. Physician assistants (PAs) assist and often substitute for primary care physicians.

Nurses

Of the 2.2 million registered nurses in the United States, approximately 400,000 are delivering primary care in a variety of settings. The shift of health care delivery to community-based sites resulted in a need for more nurses prepared to function in diverse roles. Primary care is delivered by more than 100,000 APNs—NPs (approximately 50,000), CNMs (approximately 6,000), and, increasingly, CNSs (approximately 56,000). In addition, some 300,000 other registered nurses deliver selected aspects of primary care in community and ambulatory care settings, including physicians' offices and clinics (125,000), community and public health settings (111,000), schools (48,000), and occupational health sites (22,000) (ANA 1993a, 1993b).

The increased demand for primary care has led to a call for APN educational programs to prepare increasing numbers of APNs to deliver that care (Pew 1994). Candidates for APN education are baccalaureate-prepared registered nurses (BSNs), who comprise 30 percent (almost 700,000) of all registered nurses in the United States (Division of Nursing 1993). BSNs can be prepared as primary care NPs with two additional years of full-time graduate nursing study. Post-masters primary care programs for CNSs usually can be completed in one year of full-time study. Both programs provide cost-effective preparation of primary care clinicians.

More than 300 educational programs in the United States today confer master's degrees in nursing, and fifty-one more primary care and acute care NP programs are in the planning stage. The enrollments in the graduate nursing programs have increased steadily over a five-year period, and in 1994-95, graduate enrollments increased by 10.7 percent, to almost 31,000, over the previous year (80 percent of schools reporting). Enrollment totals were 10,935 NP, 8,332 CNS, and 544 CNM students for the academic year. CNS programs generated the most graduates (2,648), followed by NP programs (1,867), and CNM programs (216) (AACN 1994).

Since 1976, the U.S. Department of Health and Human Services, through the Division of Nursing, has awarded grants to schools of nursing in APN and other areas of nursing education as well as professional nurse traineeships (Vanderbilt 1994). However, for the 1994-95 academic year, governmental funding for NP and CNM training programs totaled only $16.9 million (U.S. Senate 1994, 103-118), while an estimated $248 million was paid from Medicare funds to hospitals for acute care diploma schools of nursing (Aiken and Gwyther 1994). As the U.S. Congress continues to reduce federal spending, nursing must validate the value of advanced nursing education in terms of patient outcomes to increase funding to adequate levels.

The plethora of new NP programs has created a demand for primary care nursing faculty. Colleges are increasing the number of post-master's programs for faculty members to become primary care faculty in a timely manner

(AACN 1994; Pew 1994). With both preparations, faculty can teach APNs from a blended perspective of specialty and primary care. Also, CNS and NP faculty members together can teach and model an expanded primary care perspective and link primary care and specialty services.

Professional organizations certify APNs and accredit APN programs. Individual states generate rules and regulations that specify the educational and certification requirements for nurses in advanced practice. The National League for Nursing accredits graduate programs in nursing. The American Nurses Credentialing Center (ANCC, an ANA affiliate) certifies APNs. Since 1992, ANCC has required a master's degree for specialist exams. The National Organization of Nurse Practitioner Faculties (NONPF) and individual colleges of nursing are developing mechanisms to articulate certificate programs with master's programs to provide advanced education for these NPs (NONPF 1994). Also, NONPF published Advanced Nursing Practice: Nurse Practitioner Curriculum Guidelines and Programs Standards (NONPF 1995) to offer a standard for the development and/or revision of NP programs. Another goal for NONPF curricular guidelines is to provide guidance for both accreditation agencies and certification bodies as they evaluate NP educational programs and their graduates' competencies.

Physicians

In 1994, of the 562,500 patient care physicians, 70,500 were in family and general practice and 48,000 were general pediatricians. Of the 90,000 residencies, 7,000 were in family practice and 7,700 were in pediatrics. An additional 111,427 medical internists and 36,600 obstetrician-gynecologists provide components of primary care (Roback et al. 1994). In other developed countries, the proportion of primary care physicians is between 50 percent and 75 percent (Schroeder 1992). The Council on Graduate Medical Education [COGME] report (COGME 1992) studied the supply of primary care physicians and indicated a 50 percent increase is needed in the United States in a "predictable and timely fashion."

Federal policies toward medical education and physician reimbursement have directly encouraged preparation of specialists (Colwill 1994; Kronick, Goodman, and Wennberg 1993). The policies include generous funding for Graduate Medical Education (GME) through Medicare and Medicaid pass-throughs to hospitals for hospital-based residencies; Medicare's payment policies for hospital and physician care; and support for much more technical and biomedical research ($10 billion) than primary care research ($100 million). Between 1988 and 1992, the number of trainees in medical subspecialties grew by more than 60 percent and in specialties by 28 percent. In contrast, the number of primary care residents increased by just under 11 percent (Budetti 1994).

COGME projected an almost 25 percent increase in the overall physician-to-population ratio between 1994 and 2020. COGME recommended reforms to Congress that would change the ratio of primary care physicians to specialists from 1:2 to 1:1 (Colwill 1994). However, if reforms caused half of all graduating medical students from 1993 forward to pursue primary care residencies, the 50-50 ratio would not be reached until the year 2040 (Kindig 1994).

The cost of medical education for primary care physicians is unclear because of the complex funding formulae and aggregation of all residency funding. What has been determined is that U.S. allopathic medical schools, in the 1990–91 academic year, generated tuition, grants, and medical-service-plan fees of $22 billion. Hospitals generated Medicare and Medicaid fees for hospital-based residencies, including hospital rotations by primary care residents (Richards 1994) of $6.5 billion. In contrast, federal grant programs for the training of and support for primary-care physicians in 1993 were projected to be only $64 million (Budetti 1994).

Physician assistants

Physician Assistants (PAs) extend and substitute the physicians. They are usually governed and licensed within the medical licensing structure of the state. The PA can perform a majority of primary care tasks for individuals— the history and physical examination, diagnosis and treatment of common illnesses, and prescription of medications within guidelines. The educational foundation is predominantly medical education and therefore reflects the strengths and values of physicians—-focusing on treatment and cure of illness and also attending to general health needs. The majority of PA educational programs lead to baccalaureate degrees, with two years of general education and two years of clinical education. Upon graduation, PAs are eligible to sit for a certification exam developed by the American Medical Association. In 1992, there were 23,000 practicing PAs, most of them in ambulatory care settings. In general, the practice settings of PAs resemble those of physicians, except that greater proportion of PAs serve in rural underserved and other rural areas (PPRC 1994).

Nurses: Preferred Primary Care Clinicians

Numerous practice-based studies have indicated that nurses and physicians have common and unique knowledge, skills, and perspectives in the delivery of primary care (Brown and Grimes 1993; PPRC 1994). In 1991, the Pew Health Professions Commission surveyed practicing professionals to learn their perceptions of their educational preparation for practice. Nurses, more than the other respondents, felt that their educational programs prepared them for communicating with patients, involving patients, participating in teamwork, being sensitive to cultural diversity and community needs, and providing managed care. Physicians, more than others, felt that they were well prepared to solve problems, to diagnose and treat disease, and to engage in continuous learning. (Shugars et al. 1991). These studies support the need for more interdisciplinary training and experience of faculty, practitioners, and students to enhance complementary practice in primary care settings.

Nurses are uniquely prepared for primary care because of their beliefs, educational experiences, and client outcomes (PPRC 1994; Keane and Richmond 1993; Avorn, Everitt, and Baker 1991; Campbell et al. 1990). Nurses view clients holistically and humanistically, with an understanding and appreciation of family and community influences. Nursing education emphasizes: 1) effective communication for client teaching, support, and motivation; 2) wellness and prevention of disease or complications; 3) incorporation of client's cultural beliefs; and 4) client independence and self care. Coordination of care/case management is integral to all professional nursing. Nurses take the time for client communication needs. Nurses have demonstrated the ability to perform virtually all primary care procedures, given the instruction and opportunity to practice, and they use less invasive and expensive procedures than other clinicians (Brown and Grimes 1993).

There is significant research that shows that advanced practice nurses spend more time with patients and provide primary care that is as good as, or better than, physician care in many important measures of quality and patient satisfaction (ANA 1994). Furthermore, nurses are competent and comfortable as interdisciplinary and collaborative team members and leaders, and they are willing to experiment with different organizational models to improve care and productivity (Fagin 1990).

Graduate nursing programs for primary care blend expert nursing with knowledge from a variety of scientific arenas. APNs first earn the baccalaureate nursing degree, become licensed, and usually work as registered nurses before they enter a graduate nursing program. The two-year course of study incorporates advanced client health assessment, epidemiology, statistics, pathophysiology, pharmacology, preventive guidelines for all ages, diagnosis and management of common diseases, behavioral change strategies, and counseling and support of clients.[1] Students are taught research methods and have advanced practice with special groups, such as pregnant adolescents, low-income mothers, and/or clients with disabilities. APNs study primary care of the family and its members or specialize in primary care of women, children, adults, or the elderly. To administer managed-care systems or nursing centers, APNs earn a master's degree in nursing administration, master's degree in business administration, or an M.S.N.-M.B.A. dual degree. Increasingly, APNs also hold nursing doctoral degrees that emphasize research, administration, education, practice, or combinations of these areas of study.

Baccalaureate-prepared nurses (BSNs), prepared as generalists, provide direct health care and focus on ensuring coordinated and comprehensive care. They work collaboratively with other health care providers to manage the needs of individuals and groups (AACN 1993). The changing health care delivery system has called for a reorientation in nursing practice directed toward the provision of primary care, often within a community setting. To meet current health care needs, acute care nurses' reorientation included a shift from institution to community, individual to community group, illness to wellness, and dependent to independent functioning (Flynn 1984). These nurses will continue to play a significant role in improving access to care in many underserved areas (OTA 1986). Additional preparation at the graduate level can prepare these nurses for various roles in primary care (ANA 1993b).

Clinical nurse specialists number approximately 56,000 (ANA 1993a). CNSs provide for aspects of primary care in their care management of clients' complex and chronic illnesses. CNSs also serve as specialty care providers, consultants, and program planners within primary care settings. The CNS facilitates transitions in a person's life, particularly those between institutional and home care (Meleis and Trangenstein 1994). They are experts at making rapid, comprehensive assessments, using effective problem-solving skills in making complex clinical decisions, and acting autonomously as well as collaboratively (Haber and Billings 1993). CNS specialties include psy-

---

[1] There are educational strategies devised for adult learners to earn the equivalent of a baccalaureate degree in nursing before pursuing graduate education. Most of these learners are already practicing registered nurses or individuals with baccalaureate degrees in other fields of study.

chiatric/mental health, cardiovascular, maternal-child, community/public health, and others based on specific diseases or characteristics of populations. Besides being able to perform comprehensive health assessments and selected primary care services, these APNs provide advanced therapeutic interventions and procedures according to their specialties (Krauss 1993).

Nurse practitioners currently number approximately 50,000 (ANA 1993a). As primary care practitioners, they provide the broadest range of primary care services. NPs provide first-contact care; health assessment, health promotion, and health maintenance; and diagnosis and management of common acute and chronic illnesses; and support a dignified and comfortable death. NPs perform comprehensive physical examinations and health histories; perform or order screening and diagnostic procedures; suture minor wounds; treat common problems; and prescribe medications. NPs can provide a majority of primary care competently (OTA 1986). They use expert consultation and referral when the client problem is beyond the NP scope of practice and the individual NP's expertise.

Certified nurse-midwives number approximately 6,000 (ANA 1993a). They traditionally deliver family planning services; prenatal, intrapartum, and postnatal care; newborn and infant care; well-woman gynecological care; and perimenopausal care. While nurse-midwives take pride in their natural and low-tech approaches, they are very knowledgeable and skilled clinicians. They perform comprehensive health assessments, diagnose and treat common problems, and prescribe medications (ACNM 1992). Because of the need for more primary care, some CNMs have become interested in more general wellness and illness care of women and infants. Additionally, some educational programs are expanding their curricula to include more primary care for women throughout life.

The Research: APN and Physician Outcomes

Research on APN and physician outcomes is difficult to evaluate because comparisons take place within medical (illness/cure) and not nursing (health/self care) models; also, some methodological concerns exist (Stone 1994; Chavigny 1993). However, numerous studies have shown the positive outcomes of APN primary care, and, together, they strongly support the value of APN practice. Summaries and meta-analyses of APN studies have helped to answer questions about APN effectiveness, patient satisfaction with APN care, and joint practice issues relative to physicians (Brown and Grimes 1993;

Crosby, Ventura, and Feldman 1987; Molde and Diers 1985; OTA 1986). Several interdisciplinary studies with excellent methodology and control of biases support the value of APN practice (PPRC 1994; Avorn, Everitt, and Baker 1991; Campbell et al. 1990; Kane et al. 1989).

A study conducted by Avorn, Everitt, and Baker (1991) summarized several differences in physician and NP practice. A random sample of 501 physicians and 298 NPs responded to a vignette describing a man with epigastric pain and endoscopy showing diffuse gastritis. Respondents were able to request additional client information before recommending management of the problem. More than one-third of the physicians but only 19 percent of the NPs chose to initiate therapy without seeking relevant history. NPs asked an average of 2.6 questions while physicians asked an average of 1.6 questions. Nearly half of all physicians indicated that medication was the single most effective therapy; 65 percent recommended a histamine antagonist that had not been shown to be effective in this case. Only 20 percent of the NPs recommended a prescription medication. Physicians, more than NPs, asked about alcohol consumption and recommended reduction in alcohol intake. NPs, on the other hand, recommended a cessation of aspirin intake, over-the-counter therapy, change in diet, reduction in caffeine intake, and counseling more than their physician counterparts. This study supports the claim that nursing is different from medicine.

When APNs are at primary care sites, especially in remote areas, they meet extensive primary care needs with consultation via a variety of electronic modalities. Also, APNs have demonstrated the ability to compete successfully for managed care contracts to deliver primary care for underserved populations (Edwards 1994). Although APNs have advanced their accountability and skills, they still have very low total disclosable malpractice payments. In 1993, only eleven NPs, fourteen CNMs, and no CNSs had malpractice payments against them, according to a report from the National Practitioner Data Bank to ANA in August 1994. These data are from incidents occurring several years earlier and may represent underreporting as well as low incidence. However, nurse practitioners and nurse-midwives were responsible for a tiny fraction of all professions' payment reports from 1990 to 1993. (Birkholz 1995).

Congress requested a major review of the research literature comparing primary care clinicians such as APNs with physicians. In 1986, the OTA reported a review of conducted studies that compared NPs and physicians on a combined total of twelve patient outcome measures. They found that the care delivered by APNs was as good as, or better than, that delivered by physicians, and that NPs and CNMs are more adept than physicians in providing services that depend on communication with patients, and on preventive actions (OTA 1986, pp. 5–6). NPs achieved equivalent outcomes in four instances and better patient outcomes in eight.

Similar findings emerged from a recent meta-analysis of 38 controlled studies comparing NPs and physicians (Brown and Grimes 1993). The investigation authors compared the two professions in terms of processes of care, clinical outcomes, and/or the cost-effectiveness of resource utilization. The content of client visits was not reported and the cost of educational preparation was not a factor in cost analysis. Fifteen additional controlled studies provided data allowing CNMs and physicians to be compared on the same measures. Studies in each analysis were selected on the basis of six inclusion criteria from an initial review of 900 articles. The studies selected for inclusion in the meta-analysis represent the most scientifically rigorous research currently available comparing NP and CNM care with physician care.

The Brown and Grimes findings are consistent with those of earlier research reviews (Crosby, Ventura, and Feldman 1987; OTA 1986) and later reports (Mahoney 1994; Aiken et al. 1993) in confirming that for those variables measured, NPs and CNMs had patient outcomes equivalent to or better than those of physicians. NPs scored higher on quality of care measures (diagnostic accuracy, completeness of history-taking, and adequacy of care process) than did physicians. Meta-analysis results support observations that APNs deliberately choose to use less invasive procedures and processes of care requiring fewer resources, less expensive resources, and less technologically accelerated resources than do physicians.

Cost Analyses of APNs

Much interest in APNs has stemmed from their capacity to provide primary care that is cost-effective (OTA 1986). The term cost-effective is not merely a euphemism for less expensive or cheaper, although some analysts and researchers have emphasized this specific aspect of primary care nursing. Cost-effective care is both relatively low in cost and high in quality. The cost-effectiveness of APN care is realized by the high quality of care APNs provide coupled with the their lower educational costs and more moderate salaries when compared with physicians. This cost-effectiveness is significant, making APNs the most appropriate clinicians to provide primary care services for a variety of patient populations. A new method of costing services, activity-based costing, will reveal much more about real costs of an advanced nursing service, such as total costs related to case management of an elderly client with diabetes mellitus (Case 1995). The increased accuracy of this process undoubtedly will reveal the cost savings of APNs who manage clients holistically, use "telepractice" to consult with specialists and to support clients at home, and make home visits to provide care as necessary.

The W. K. Kellogg Foundation reported studies comparing APN and generalist physician costs as primary care clinicians (Boex et al. 1993). First, all primary care clinicians were found to be more cost-effective than physician specialists. Second, in five cited studies, the APN costs ranged from 60 percent to 83 percent of physician costs, excluding the cost of educational preparation. To emphasize further the extent of APN cost-effectiveness, the Kellogg Foundation compared a set of charges for an initial visit for a headache: $75 by the APN, $125 by the primary care physician, and $235 by the neurologist.

Considering an APN only as a physician substitute does not measure all of the client benefits of advanced practice nursing. However, several of these studies indicated that APNs could perform from 50 percent to 75 percent of the tasks performed by physicians caring for adults and 90 percent of those performed by physicians caring for children at the time the studies were done (OTA 1986). Globally, the OTA estimates that substituting APNs for physicians would result in equivalent client outcomes and could save 10 percent—15 percent of total medical expenditures and up to 25 percent of the costs of ambulatory care. To determine the current costs of underutilization of nurses, Nichols (1992) analyzed the savings if APNs were to substitute for physicians. This study calculated that the cost of underutilization of APNs ranged from 5.5 percent to 7.5 percent of total health expenditures. Economic analyses are not complete for many APN services, but the great demand for APN services (Pew 1994) strongly suggests that they are cost-effective.

CNS outcome studies, comparing their care with that of physicians, have not undergone meta-analyses yet, probably because many of their activities are uniquely nursing. However, CNSs studies have shown excellent outcomes and substantial savings by providing care that interfaces with or includes aspects of primary care in conjunction with specialty care. CNSs have reduced premature births in high-risk pregnant women, prevented hospitalization of the elderly with arthritis, and enabled early discharge of low birthweight infants (Alverson 1994; Anderson 1994; Brooten et al. 1986). Baradell (1994) found that the psychiatric mental health CNS (PMHCNS) in North

Carolina charged fees 19 percent to 35 percent lower than the fees charged by psychiatrists and psychologists and had equivalent or better patient outcomes. Psychiatric clients who enrolled in a symptom management course developed and presented by PMHCNS experienced 85 percent decreased hospitalization, at savings of $9,347 per client (Moller 1994).

Outcome/cost studies for nurses prepared at the baccalaureate level practicing in primary care are usually related to nurses with additional training and experience, as in school nursing and occupational health nursing, and are not within the scope of this monograph. However, nurses prepared at the basic level are often the only clinicians in many community health settings and thus provide a range of care, referring the client to an APN or physician as necessary. Also, in many public health settings for underserved populations and in primary care clinicians' offices, baccalaureate-prepared nurses work closely with the primary care team to provide quality care within the legal scope of practice for a registered nurse.

Barriers to Practice

Beginning in the late 1970s, federal and state laws increasingly recognized APNs as primary care clinicians. In some states, APNs own and manage freestanding facilities and consult with physicians and other professionals to provide a full range of primary care services. However, many barriers still prevent APNs from full participation in primary care delivery (Safreit 1992). Restrictive nurse practice acts, unnecessary supervision, lack of prescriptive authority, reimbursement barriers, malpractice insurance costs and restrictions, and lack of institutional privileges constrain their practice (ANA 1994). Managed care systems often refuse to consider successful APN practices for capitated primary care contracts, thereby restricting the practice of these clinicians. Medicare will reimburse APNs in rural areas, but if the area becomes too populous to be categorized as rural, the APN becomes ineligible for reimbursement. (Segal-Issacson 1994). Present regulations and policies often allow client entry to primary care via the physician as the first and only provider and thereby delay, postpone, or deny care by APNs (Sekscenski et al. 1994).

Nurses have employed several strategies to remove barriers to their primary care practice. Nurses have organized at local, state, regional, and national levels to change legislation and regulations, form coalitions with consumer groups, improve APNs public image, market APN services to corporate

America, and provide services in areas with shortages. Individual APNs have negotiated for practice spaces as established, sanctioned physician practices, while others have migrated to friendlier environments. Colleges of nursing have developed faculty practices from which to negotiate delivery of scholarly practice to various populations and types of markets. Nurse researchers have conducted studies to show the positive outcomes of APNs and disseminated the findings. In spite of formidable barriers, APNs are in increasing demand (Pew 1995).

Summary

While there is a maldistribution of primary care in the United States, nursing has made great strides in preparing nurses for various primary care roles. Advanced practice nurses are the preferred primary care providers for many populations, especially the poor, people with disabilities, and minorities. Graduate nursing programs prepare APNs to communicate with patients, involve patients, participate in collaborative teams, be culturally competent and sensitive to community needs, and function in managed care systems. Also, nurses use low-tech methods and a self-care approach. Even with the numerous barriers to APN practice, utilization of APNs is growing and the increased demand for APN primary care education is being addressed (Pew 1994, 1995).

❊ *Recommendation 2*

Provide for an adequate workforce of primary care providers.

- Increase educational support for primary care, multicultural, and community-based training of health professionals.
- Establish new funding to support graduate primary care nursing education.
- Support collaborative interdisciplinary primary care training programs.
- Remove practice barriers for APNs and other qualified primary care providers.

Quality, Cost-Effective Health Care System for the United States

3

The health care delivery system will consume more than one-seventh of the U.S. gross domestic product in the mid-1990s (Burner, Waldo, and McKusick 1992). Costs continue to rise, yet our health outcomes are not as good as other developed countries (Scheiber, Poullier, and Greenwald 1994). The United States urgently needs a logical, fiscally sound, integrated system of health care and health coverage for all people. Health care coverage should not only include but should reward primary care and preventive services. By developing multiple strategies utilizing public/private partnerships to finance health care, the costs can be shared with less impact on any one segment of society.

Within the framework of quality and cost-effective care for all people, diverse and innovative providers and approaches to care are necessary to deliver and finance primary care across populations. Because of the diversity among Americans, a single delivery model cannot address the health needs of all of the nation's people. Also, any new delivery system must attend to the health needs of forty million uninsured people in this country. To achieve quality and cost-effectiveness and adapt to various diverse populations, nursing supports three broad changes in the structure of the U.S. health care system:

- Development of a decentralized network for primary care delivery system.
- Creation of comprehensive integrated health care delivery systems based on the decentralized primary care system.
- Revitalization of the U.S. public health system.

A Decentralized Delivery Network

Nursing recommends the creation of a dense, nationwide network of existing and new small-scale primary care centers. The centers should reflect World Health Organization (WHO 1978) community-oriented approaches to care. These client- and family-centered, convenient, and familiar local facilities would link with components of other community health and social systems. The centers would contract with comprehensive systems to serve as sites for members and beneficiaries of health maintenance organizations, preferred provider organizations, point-of-service, Medicare, Medicaid, Federal Employee Benefits Program, public health programs, or one large integrated delivery system.

Primary care delivery models can and should have a low economic impact, offering the most frequently needed services where people live and where they spend their lives. Additionally, some essential but infrequently needed services, such as speech therapy and podiatry, can be delivered intermittently as part of comprehensive primary care services. Because clients of all ages can receive care at a neighborhood primary care site, the entire family may attend the same facility and see the same clinician. Typically, primary care offices and centers are owned and staffed by physicians, hospitals, academic health centers, and public health departments. Too often, these facilities are sparsely distributed and loosely connected, especially the hospital and academic health center clinics where poor people often receive care. Physicians' offices and public health centers have not filled the geographic gaps in the health care network. Recently, new primary care delivery models have emerged with centers, satellites, and linkages forged by advanced practice nurses (APNs) and other clinicians.

Models of Care

Neighborhood health centers

The neighborhood health centers (NHC) model reflects the WHO primary health care philosophy and encourages the community to take part in its development. The model removes barriers to care and focuses on empowering residents to assume responsibility for their own care. Primary care delivered in familiar settings offers clients a sense of belonging. Because the NHC offers outreach efforts and community-oriented care, residents are more active participants in their care. The conventional NHC model has extended beyond the neighborhood health center into schools, churches, suburban shopping malls, mobile vans, small grass-roots niches such as storefront health centers, high-rise business districts, industrial parks, and workplaces. Primary care can be delivered to children, teenagers, adults, families, and the elderly where they live and spend their lives. Neighborhood health centers were first funded by the Economic Opportunity Act of 1964 (Holthaus 1993) and now are supported jointly by local, state, federal, and private funds.

Nursing centers

The first documented nursing center was the Henry Street Settlement, established by Lillian Wald in New York City in 1893 (Wald 1934; Coss 1992). Mary Breckinridge founded the Frontier Nursing Service in the mountains of Kentucky; she opened the first nursing center in 1925 and six more centers by 1930 (Holthaus 1993). The Community Nursing Centers Act of 1983 defined and funded nurse-managed centers (Capan, Beard, and Mashburn 1993). Nursing centers have reemerged as academic, non-profit, charitable, and proprietary clinics, primarily as a nursing response to the needs of underserved populations. Advanced practice nurses (APNs) own and manage solo and group private and primary care practices in several states (Levin 1993; Sullivan et al. 1993). Nurse practitioners (NPs) compete with other primary care providers for clients and for contracts with managed-care corporations, federal and state agencies, businesses, hospital emergency departments, schools, and other entities needing primary care delivery. Clinical nurse specialists (CNSs), particularly those in psychiatric mental health care, have long had private practices delivering individual, family, and group psychotherapy; prescribing medications; providing and coordinating care; establishing networks of support; and offering a variety of other services (Haber and Billings 1993).

Nursing centers throughout the nation have provided an alternative to medical primary care. Academic and nonacademic centers total about 300 centers (Barger and Rosenfeld 1993; Holthaus 1993). However, there is no reliable accounting of the numerous satellite clinics run by nurses but owned by state and federal public health departments, hospitals, physicians, and other agencies throughout the nation. These centers provide services by APNs who collaborate with physicians and others as necessary. Most of these centers offer a full range of primary care (Capan, Beard, and Mashburn 1993). Furthermore, nurse-directed centers provide individual and group services consistent with community need. An example of a successful nursing center can be found in the rural South:

In December 1993, the Family Health Center in Sumter, S.C., opened its doors with NPs as clinicians. The center is managed by Sue Scouter, MN, RN, CS, a family nurse practitioner and community nurse specialist. Owned by the Tuomey Regional Medical Center, the facility is both a community alternative to inappropriate use of the emergency department and the only source of primary care for most of the county's poor. In the last fifteen years, the Sumter County population increased from 23,000 to 42,000, but the number of physicians decreased by one. None of the county primary care physicians—family practice, pediatric, or ob/gyn—accepted clients with Medicaid coverage.

After two years, the NPs had 30,000 client visits and the client base approached 10,000. Their clientele includes about seventy individuals with HIV/AIDS, school children with myriad special needs, clients from the BEST CHANCE program that screens for breast and cervical cancer, clients with common acute and chronic illnesses, and clients with nonemergent problems who were triaged and referred by the emergency department.

While full-range primary care services are covered by Medicaid at the Family Health Center, services to family members who are Medicare beneficiaries are not covered. Federal reimbursement regulations relative to Medicare reimbursement support NPs only in rural areas or "incident to" physician services. The center anxiously awaits health care reform of Medicare regulations to cover NP services in populated, not just rural, areas. In the meantime, the NPs see a need for satellite clinics in the rural parts of the county where public transportation is nonexistent. They plan to provide linkages with the school system and other agencies with underserved groups in the greater Sumter community. The center also serves as a major practice site for NP faculty and a training site for NP graduate students from the University of South Carolina College of Nursing.

Schools and colleges

For decades, school and college health nurses have provided components of primary care. To improve the health of children, federal and state initiatives have provided nursing services for families in neighborhood schools. In colleges, student health services are available. These centers range from full service primary care sites for a managed-care system paid by student insurance to a referral center. In 1992, 7.2 percent of all practicing NPs served in student health services (PPRC 1994).

The first of many school-based health programs was established in Dallas in 1970 (Center for Populations Options 1988). Adolescents, a high-risk, underserved population, have utilized school-based clinics for many health needs (Falsetti and Kovel 1994). Colorado, Florida, Kentucky, and New Jersey are piloting a model that expands the role of schools, allowing them to function as broad, multiservice human resource facilities in their communities. In addition to primary care, these centers include such programs as job training for parents, parenting skills, legal aid, and social services. School-based primary care clinics may increase the immunization levels of the school child's preschool siblings. Clearly, APNs and school nurses economically and appropriately avoid unnecessary duplication of services (Igoe and Giordano 1992).

Health centers for college students may have a lone NP or a large team of primary care clinicians. In larger schools, more services are available, including diagnostic studies and overnight facilities. In nurse-managed centers, the philosophy tends to be more wellness-directed, with the emphasis being on health promotion, disease prevention, and self care, as well as the early detection and prompt treatment of illness, An annual assessment of the campus needs and community resources is necessary for planning, primarily for individuals and aggregates with sexually transmitted diseases, disabilities, mental health needs, and other concerns. To provide continuity of services, the primary care clinician refers to a variety of college and community facilities (Novinger 1992). The college health center has been a logical and convenient place for NP educational programs to establish practice opportunities for their faculty and students.

Home care services

Home care nurses have delivered personal health care to residents in their homes for at least a century. A variety of home care services are now available, including social services, occupational and other therapies, and home care aides. Countless programs permit elderly persons to remain in their homes with appropriate primary care services available to them. Most chronic illnesses, when not in acute exacerbation, can be managed in the home setting, thus preventing unnecessary complications that often occur in institutional settings. Ongoing visits to assure elder safety through environmental modifications are very inexpensive compared with the costs of fractures due to falls, hospitalization, and long-term rehabilitation. However, supportive and preventive measures within home care have been the least supported by health care policy and insurance benefits (Burner, Waldo, and McKusick 1992).

Churches

Nurses have expanded parish nursing to include direct care. Provision of care takes place in church-based clinics and parishioner's homes, and it may include hospital visits as well. The great advantage parish nurses have is that of knowing and being known by parishioners and their families, and of becoming known by people in the church's community. Parish nurses provide health assessment, primary care, crisis intervention and pastoral care, and follow-up visits to new mothers. These services minimize the impact of illness and maximize the potential for health within a given population. In underserved areas, such as rural communities or the inner city, parish nursing offers a model of accessibility and efficiency for delivery of care to those who need it most.

Work sites

Occupational health services have traditionally focused on the prevention and management of work-related illness and injury. Corporate and other employers have gained an increased appreciation for the relationships between personal health status, family health status, safe and healthy workplaces, and an individual's capacity for productivity and innovative contribution. Many employers are beginning to see in-house health care delivery systems with nurse-managed primary care clinics as a means to deliver high quality care while reducing costs (Burgel 1992). More employers are instituting work-site programs that offer services to which employees would otherwise have no access, as well as programs that improve the health status of the employee, such as smoking cessation and physical fitness.

In 1993, approximately 20,000 registered nurses were employed in work-site health settings (Division of Nursing 1993). While the actual number of nurses in occupational health nursing is unknown, at least 700 NPs have allied with the American Association of Occupational Health Nursing, according to the association's director of governmental affairs. Services offered by these nurses include health education, prevention, and early intervention. In many settings, primary care services extend to include all levels of prevention, an emphasis on occupational health and safety, and the education of employees regarding self-care, health promotion, and the appropriate use of resources. Case management is used to monitor utilization of services, including workers compensation claims (ANF 1993). Cost-effective work site health care delivered by occupational health nurses are described in the following examples:

In a 1988 study, 42 percent of Northern Telecom health center visits were for primary care; 37 percent dealt with occupational injury. Net cost savings and benefits from this in-house primary and occupational health care service were estimated to be more than $2.4 million annually. The company experienced a 40 percent decline in lost work days, annual decreases in accident frequency and severity, and a 50 percent improvement in internal safety audits (Dalton and Harris 1991).

At Hickory Hill Furniture Corp. in Valdese, N.C., the nurse practitioner provided the most primary care services for the worker and the worker's family at the worksite. The nurse had a collaborative relationship with a family physician who acted as a consultant and who would see patients with complex medical problems. With health expenditures per year per employee in the United States averaging almost $4,000, this worksite averaged $1,258 in 1992. In late 1994, costs were 58 percent below the 1993 average (Zentner et al. 1995).

The Marriott Corporation depends on the expertise of nurses in its claims offices, in nursing centers, and on the hotel properties. Since 1992, a nurse practitioner in a freestanding clinic has served 2,000 hotel employees in the Phoenix area. Each program has significant savings. Each nurse in claims management saves $250,000 per year and each nursing center saves more than $260,000 per year (ANF 1993).

Long-term care and residential facilities

The health care of dependent people living in group facilities often has been a shameful deficiency in our society. Individuals in residences who are retarded, elderly, mentally ill, homeless, or incarcerated often receive a low standard of care. There are numerous reports of poor medical care in nursing homes, jails, and mental institutions (Wilson and Leasure 1991; Kane et al. 1989; Droes 1985). When nurses enter these systems, they bring a humanistic and caring approach along with their quality primary care skills. As nurses, they demonstrate the ability to work well in collaborative, interdisciplinary teams, attributes supported by the Robert Wood Johnson Foundation's teaching nursing home project (Mezey and Lynaught 1991). They use a broader system of care characterized by referrals and, in some cases, hospital care. Nurse-managed systems in long-term care and residential facilities are also potential primary care sites for managed-care systems.

Primary Care within a Comprehensive Integrated Health System

The comprehensive integrated health care delivery system (IDS) is a multiservice expansion of the classic health maintenance organization. The IDS offers a vertically and horizontally integrated continuum of services, clinicians, and strategically placed facilities. All points are connected by an electronic information and revenue transfer system, taking care to protect client confidentiality. Primary, secondary, and tertiary care services are coordinated, usually from the decentralized primary care network. Primary care services are provided from a network of neighborhood-based centers that offer preventive programs. Other primary care services include acute and chronic disease management, case management in all areas, and counseling and psychiatric/mental health services. With acute episodes of illnesses, the system may provide coordination of secondary and tertiary care via the expertise of an APN, e.g., an oncology CNS. An IDS may provide an in-house birthing center, home care, hospice, rehabilitative services, and long-term care. Client transitions from setting to setting are carefully coordinated. All health care settings provide supervision for dependent elders and children, so caregivers can visit the clinician alone.

Comprehensive systems compete for clients on the basis of quality, cost, and accessibility of care. They have the capacity to serve large and diverse client populations. The services may be reimbursed through a variety of public, private employer-funded, and/or personal funding mechanisms, with different payment schemes. The IDS provides care for managed care health systems. A standardized, per-person annual "capitation" fee is paid for all health and illness care for most clients. Capitation serves as an incentive to provide quality primary care services and to avoid unnecessary specialty and hospital care, but this method reduces choice of providers, treatments, and medications. The primary care clinician is a coordinator of services. The IDS also provides services on a fee-for-service basis for clients who are self-pay or have indemnity insurance.

Any comprehensive health care organization must be designed to provide access to services while maintaining an individualized approach to care. Because an IDS is a large bureaucracy that holds productivity as a major goal, care must be taken not to insulate clinicians from their clients or to treat the client as a commodity or profit center.

A Revitalized Public Health System

In its 1988 publication The Future of Public Health, the Institute of Medicine (IOM) Committee for the Study of the Future of Public Health concluded that "this nation has lost sight of its public health care goals and has allowed the system of public health activities to fall into disarray" (IOM 1988, p. 1). The public health system is vast and has assumed an exploding number of responsibilities—most specifically the provision of hands-on direct care for those rejected by the health care delivery system (Salmon 1993).

The public health system traditionally has focused on resolving problems of a national or community scope, and the nation has needed primary care. However, when the majority of public health funds are being spent on delivery of direct personal care services, there are insufficient funds to address broader health issues. These might include the need to eradicate communicable diseases, to prevent disease such as through smoking cessation campaigns, and the pressing demand for more health data for better planning.

In July 1990, the Senate Committee on Labor and Human Resources passed the Health Objectives 2000 Act. In so doing, it recommended that the nation's public health system be revitalized. The Committee acknowledged that the public health system's ability to maintain and improve the quality of American life has been hampered severely by lack of resources, inadequate infrastructure, and insufficient coordination between governmental levels. The committee endorsed recommendations put forth in The Future of Public Health: that the federal government take decisive steps to fulfill the following public health obligations:

- To support public health knowledge development and dissemination through data gathering, research, and information exchange;
- To establish nationwide health objectives and priorities, and to stimulate debate on interstate and national public health issues;
- To provide technical assistance to help states and localities determine their own objectives and to act on national and regional objectives; and
- To provide funds to states to strengthen their capacity to deliver services— especially to attain adequate minimum capacity—and to achieve national health objectives.

In the report accompanying the Health Objectives 2000 Act, the committee urged federal support for an increased emphasis on health promotion and disease prevention. It also authorized funding for this purpose, rising in increments to reach $400 million by 1995. While this figure represented a significant increase in federal support for preventive programs, the committee described it as a "modest and wise investment when current health care expenditures and the cost-effectiveness of preventive services are considered." The committee pointed out that the appropriation amounted to only $1.25 per person, per year, although at that time health care for the average American cost well over $2,500 per year.

Nursing believes that public health revitalization should be approached by assuring that all people have personal health care within the decentralized primary care system. The resulting leaner, more vital public health system then will be able to focus on issues concerning the nation's health from a population and environmental perspective (Aiken and Salmon 1994). The new system will need a new image, consistent with its mission of fostering and maintaining the nation's health.

A new public health system should develop a unified, coherent health care policy to promote national health care goals throughout the delivery system. Policy supporting primary care and other public health preventive strategies should be clearly, rationally, and consistently defined in relation to specialty care. Health policy should be an interwoven part of a logically designed national policy affecting the general welfare of all the people.

To benefit national health policy, we need more meaningful national health surveillance, nationwide information linkages, data analysis, and outcomes research. The development of a nationwide health database and linkage system would allow for the multiple elements of the health care system to share, process, and disseminate information at all levels of operation. Such linkage would enable researchers, policy-makers, and regional planners to see the broad health picture. Furthermore, public health research should strengthen primary care by developing more research-based guidelines for the management of specific, common primary care problems. Cost-effective approaches to primary care practice are especially needed.

The new public health system will need to provide technical assistance to public health clinics during the transition to full service in the decentralized primary care network. Public health professionals can support start-up efforts with clinical guidelines, expertise, and grant funding. Ability to work on cost-effective, qualified, and collaborative multidisciplinary teams is one of the major strengths that public health workers will bring to primary care settings. Conversely, some seasoned public health personal care clinicians will need assistance in designing and implementing population-based interventions.

The United States must develop and promote primary preventive campaigns at the national level, utilizing national and local media and every part of the decentralized primary care network. Health promotion campaign also may be targeted to selected states, cities, and neighborhoods, according to specific risks. For example, smoking cessation programs may use T.V., billboards, flyers, and radio to reach at-risk adolescents. The public health industry also will need more research in social marketing to understand better how to improve the image and value of health promotive behaviors among high-risk populations.

Outreach for vulnerable populations will continue to be a public health focus. Outreach includes case-finding, counseling, education, and referral programs for risk groups at the local level. Teen-age pregnancy, substance abuse, family violence or sexual abuse, trauma from rape, poor quality of life for the elderly, and communicable diseases are among the numerous problems that will remain within the public health domain. However, with public health coordination and assistance, the decentralized primary care delivery system will in time be able to provide more services to counter these problems.

The public health system will need to support the public health and primary care education of epidemiologists, biostatisticians, environmental and occupational health specialists, nutritionists, basic and advanced practice nurses, physicians, and others. There is a continuing need to emphasize the recruitment and training of minority public health professionals and those serving in rural and other underserved areas. The education of public health and primary care professionals should be interdisciplinary, with shared learning and clinical experiences.

Summary

Nursing proposes the development of a decentralized primary care delivery system and the creation of comprehensive integrated delivery systems (IDSs) for the care of all people. Nurses are well-qualified to deliver primary care, work in interdisciplinary and collaborative teams, and manage primary care centers. Financing the health care system should be done by public and private partnerships. As personal care is transferred to IDSs, the U.S. public health system should undergo revitalization. The newly organized health care delivery system should reflect nursing's beliefs that quality primary care is client-centered, coordinated, current, and accessible. The revitalized public health system should support the primary care delivery system but focus on population and environmentally-based health objectives.

❊ *Recommendation 3*

Establish a method of primary care delivery for all people.
- Provide health care coverage that includes primary care and preventive services, starting with those at the beginning of life and then other vulnerable uninsured populations.
- Develop multiple strategies utilizing public/private partnerships to finance health care coverage.
- Restructure health care financing to reward primary and preventive care.

Recommendation 4

Develop public and private partnerships to create a new structure for health care delivery.

- Build a new system with primary care as the broad and stable base.
- Develop a dense, decentralized, community-oriented primary care delivery network with numerous sites in areas where people live and work.
- Create integrated delivery systems that provide comprehensive. coordinated services.
- Revitalize the U.S. public health system to address public health policy, health promotion and disease prevention; conduct research and health surveillance; and form public/private partnerships to deliver health care and share technical expertise.
- Develop multiple strategies utilizing public/private partnerships to finance health care for all people.

CONCLUSION

As health care expenditures soar to 15 percent of the gross domestic product, the nation clearly must contain those costs. High health care costs for the sick, uninsured, and underinsured people without regular health care burdens the nation. The pattern of health care for the insured has been to cure illness with expensive specialty care rather than to pay for prevention and early treatment with primary care. These patterns were maintained by economic and political forces and public policy. However, the corporate world and state and federal governments have implemented rapid and dramatic managed care for a majority of the insured people. With these changes, there will be much less cost-shifting to pay for uninsured individuals. Ultimately, businesses, governments, and other forces will be forced to negotiate partnerships to provide basic health care for more, if not all, people.

The belief in health care for all people and a caring, humanistic yet ecologic, and practical philosophy are basic to nursing's proposal for primary care. A decentralized primary care system should be the foundation for a comprehensive integrated health system. APNs, often working in interdisciplinary, collaborative teams but also alone and in nursing groups, should be recognized and utilized as preferred primary care clinicians for many, particularly vulnerable, populations. APNs also can provide the "glue" for the system by giving and coordinating complex and/or long-term care. Finally, the public health system needs to be freed from the responsibility of personal health care to pursue health goals for the nation as a whole.

REFERENCES

Aiken, L. H., and Gwyther, M. 1994. *Medicare funding of nurse and paramedical education: Final report*. University of Pennsylvania, PA: Center for Health Services and Policy Research.

Aiken, L. H., Lake, E. T., Semaan, S., Lehman, H.P., O'Hare, P. A., Cole, C. S., Dunbar, D., and Frank, I. 1993. Nurse practitioner managed care for persons with HIV infection. *IMAGE: Journal of Nursing Scholarship, 25*(3): 172–177.

Aiken, L. H., and Salmon, M. 1994. Health care workforce priorities: What nursing should do now. *Inquiry, 31*: 318–329.

Alpert, J. J., and Charney, E. 1973. *The education of physicians for primary care* (Publication No. HRA 74–3113). Washington, DC: U.S. Department of Health Education Welfare.

Alverson, D. 1994, July. *On the outside looking in—the role and image of the APN in the real world*. Paper presented at the meeting of the American Association of Colleges and Nursing and American Organization of Nurse Executives, Santa Fe, NM.

American Academy of Nursing (AAN). 1976. *Primary care by nurses: sphere of responsibility and accountability*. Kansas City, MO: American Nurses Association.

American Association of Colleges of Nursing (AACN). 1993. *Nursing education's agenda for the Twenty-first century*. Washington, DC: Author.

———. 1994. *Nursing school enrollments continue steady climb*. Washington, DC: Author.

American College of Nurse-Midwives. (ACNM). 1992. Nurse-midwives historically key answer to maternal health care problem. *Facts* (PR92–10/23). Washington, DC: Author.

American Nurses Association (ANA). 1985. *The scope of practice of the primary health care nurse practitioner*. Kansas City, MO: Author.

————. *1987. Standards of practice for the primary health care nurse practitioner. Kansas City, MO: Author.*

————. *1993a. Advanced practice nursing: A new age in health care.* Washington DC: Author.

————. 1993b. *Primary health care: The nurse solution.* Washington DC: Author.

————. 1994. *Nurses win greater role under Clinton Health Plan.* Washington, DC: Author.

American Nurses Foundation (ANF). 1993. *America's nurses: Business solutions for health care delivery.* Washington, DC: American Nurses Association.

Anderson, R. 1994, July. *Acute care practitioners reach beyond the walls. Paper presented at the meeting of the American Association of Colleges of Nursing and the American Organization of Nurse Executives, Santa Fe, NM.*

Avorn, J., Everitt, D., and Baker, M. 1991. The neglected medical history and therapeutic choices for abdominal pain: A nationwide study of 799 physicians and nurses. Archives of Internal Medicine, 151(4): 694–698.

Barger, S., and Rosenfeld, P. 1993. Models in community health care: Findings from a national study of community nursing centers. *Nursing & Health Care, 14*(8): 426–431.

Baradell, J. 1994. Cost-effectiveness and quality of care provided by clinical nurse specialists. *Journal of Psychosocial Nursing, 32*(3): 21–24.

Barnes, D., Eribes, C., Juarbe, T., Nelson, M., Proctor, S., Sawyer, L., Shaul, M., and Meleis, A. 1995. Primary health care and primary care: A confusion of philosophies. *Nursing Outlook, 43*(1): 7–16.

Birkholtz, G. 1985. Malpractice data from the national practitioner data bank. *Nursing Outlook, 43*(1): 7–16.

————. 1995. National data from the National Practitioner Data Bank. *The Nurse Practitioner: The American Journal of Primary Health Care, 20*(3): 32–35.

Boex, J. R., Garg, M., Edwards, J., Marder, W. D., and Politzer, R. 1993. *Primary care practitioners: Analyses of competencies, costs, quality of care, and effects of training upon supply.* A Report Prepared for the W. K. Kellogg Foundation.

Brooten, D., Kumar, S., Brown, L., Butts, P., Finkler, S., Bakewell-Sachs, S., Gibbons, A., and Delivoria-Papadapoulos, M. 1986. A randomized clinical trial of early discharge and home follow up of very low birthweight infants. *The New England Journal of Medicine, 315*: 934–939.

Brown, S. A., and Grimes, D. E. 1993. *A meta-analysis of process of care, clinical outcome, and cost-effectiveness of nurses in primary care roles: Nurse practitioners and certified nurse midwives.* Prepared for the American Nurses Association Division of Health Policy.

Budetti, P.P. 1994, March 8. "Training health professionals for a new health system." Testimony to the U.S. Senate Committee on Finance.

Burgel, B. J. 1992. *Innovation at the worksite: Delivery of nurse-managed primary health care services.* Washington, DC: American Nurses Publishing.

Burner, S. T., Waldo, D. R., and McKusick, D. R. 1992. National health expenditures projections through 2030. *Health Care Financing Review, 14*(1): 1–57.

Campbell, J. D., Mauksch, H. O., Neikirk, H. J., and Hosokawa, M. C. 1990. Collaborative practice and provider styles of delivering health care. *Soc. Sci. Med., 30*(12): 1359–1365.

Capan, P., Beard, M., and Mashburn, M. 1993. Nurse-managed clinics provide access and improved health care. *Nurse Practitioner, 18*(5): 50–55.

Case, J. 1995. Activity-based costing crucial under managed care. *Managed Home Care, 2*(12):185–193.

Center for Population Options. 1988. *School-based clinics: A guide for advocates.* Washington, DC: Author.

Chavigny, K. 1993. AMA's policies and nursing's role in emerging systems. *Nursing Management, 24*(12): 30–34.

Children's Defense Fund. 1990. *Report on 1989 maternal and child health federal legislation.* Washington, DC: Author.

Council on Graduate Medical Education (COGME). 1992. *Council on graduate medical education, third report* (PHS, DHHS). Washington, DC: Author.

Colwill, J. M. 1994, March 8. "Recommendations to improve health care access, cost and quality through physician workforce reform." Testimony to U.S. Senate Committee on Finance.

Coss, C. 1992. Lillian D. Wald: Progressive activist. *Public Health Nursing, 10*(2): 134–138.

Crandall, E. P. 1993. The relation of public health nursing to the public health campaign. *Public Health Nursing, 10*(3): 204–209.

Crosby, F., Ventura, M. R., and Feldman, M. J. 1987. Future research recommendations for establishing NP effectiveness. *Nurse Practitioner, 12*: 75–79.

Dalton, B. A., and Harris, J. S. 1991. A comprehensive approach to corporate health management. *Journal of Occupational Medicine, 33*(3): 338–347.

Davis, E. O. 1993. Establishing a nurse-managed center: Assuring excellence. *Nurse Practitioner Forum, 4*(3): 151–157.

Davis, K., Bialek, R., Parkinson, M., Smith, J., and Vellozzi, C. 1990. Paying for preventive care: Moving the debate forward. New York: Oxford Press for the *American Journal of Preventive Medicine, 6*(4): Supplement 1–32.

DeAngelis, C. D. 1994. Nurse practitioner redux.. *Journal of the American Medical Association, 217*(11): 868–871.

De Lew, N., Greenberg, G., and Kinchen, K. 1992. A layman's guide to the U.S. health care system. *Health Care Financing Review, 14*(1): 151–169.

Dickey, L. L. 1993, January. Promoting preventive care with patient-held minirecords: A review. *Patient Education and Counseling, 20*(1): 37.

Division of Nursing. 1993. *The registered nurse population: Findings from the National Sample Survey of Registered Nurses,* March 1992 (preliminary). Washington, DC: USDHHS, Bureau of Health Professions.

Droes, N. 1985. Community health nurses in correctional settings. *Community health nursing* (pp. 418–437), edited by Archer, S., and Fleshman, R.. Monterey, CA: Wadsworth Health Sciences.

Edwards, J. B. 1994. Achieving family nurse practitioner care for an Appalachian community. *NP News*, *2*(1):1 and 4.

Erkel, E. A. 1993. The impact of case management in preventive services. *Journal of Nursing Administration*, *23*(1): 27–32.

Fagin, C.M. March, 1990. *Nurses managing the challenge of cost containment: Long term care, and more.* Paper presented at the meeting of the National Commission on Nursing Implementation Project Conference, Palm Springs, CA.

———. 1993. Primary care as an academic discipline. *Nurses, nurse practitioners* (pp. 88–101), edited by Mezey, M. P., and McGivern, D. O.. New York: Springer Publishing Company.

Falsetti, D., and Kovel, A. 1994. How one school-based clinic is meeting the challenge of adolescent health care. *Journal of the American Academy of Nurse Practitioners*, *6*(8): 363–368.

Flynn, B. C. 1984. Public health nursing education for primary health care. *Public Health Nursing*, *1*(1): 36–44.

Griffith, H. M. 1994. Resources to put more prevention into your practice. *Journal of the American Academy of Nurse Practitioners*, *6*(6): 253–256.

Haber, J. and Billings, C.V. 1993. Primary mental health care: A vision for the future of psychiatric-mental health nursing. *ANA Council Perspectives*, *2*(2): 1.

Holthaus, R. 1993. Nurse-managed health care: An ongoing tradition. *Nurse Practitioner Forum*, *4*(3): 128–132.

Igoe, J., and Giordano. B. 1992. *Expanding school health services to serve families in the Twenty-first century.* Washington, DC: American Nurses Association.

Institute of Medicine. 1978. Primary care in medicine: A definition. Chap. 2 in *A manpower policy for primary health care: Report of a study.* Washington, DC: National Academy Press.

———. 1984. *Community oriented primary care: A practical assessment: Vol. 1.* The committee report. Washington, DC: National Academy Press.

———. 1988. *The future of public health.* Washington, DC: National Academy Press.

———. 1994. *Defining primary care: An interim report.* Washington, DC: National Academy Press.

Kane, R. L., Garrard, J., Skay, C. L., Radosevich, D. M., Buchanan, J. L., McDermott, S. M., Arnold, S. B., and Kepferle, L. 1989. Effects of a geriatric nurse practitioner on process and outcome of nursing home care. *American Journal of Public Health*, *79*(9): 1271–1277.

Keane, A., and Richmond, T. 1993. Tertiary nurse practitioners. *IMAGE: Journal of Nursing Scholarship*, *25*(4): 281–284.

Kindig, D. A. 1994. Counting generalist physicians. *Journal of the American Medical Association*, *271*(19): 1505–1507.

Krauss, J. 1993. *Health care reform: Essential mental health services.* Washington DC: American Nurses Publishing.

Kronick, R., Goodman, D.C., and Wennberg, J. 1993. The marketplace in health care reform: The demographic limitations of managed competition. *New England Journal of Medicine, 328*(2): 148–152.

Levin, T. E. 1993. The solo nurse practitioner: A private practice model. *Nurse Practitioner Forum, 4*(3): 158–164.

Lewy, R. M. 1977. The emergence of the family practitioner: An historical analysis of a new specialty. *Journal of Medical Education, 52*: 873–881.

Mahoney, D. F. 1994. Appropriateness of geriatric prescribing decisions made by nurse practitioners and physicians. *IMAGE: Journal of Nursing Scholarship, 26*(1): 41–46.

McElmurry, B. 1994. *Primary health care. Center for the study of primary health care.* Chicago, IL: University of Illinois at Chicago College of Nursing.

McGinnis, J. M., and Foege, W. H. 1993. Actual causes of death in the United States. *Journal of the American Medical Association, 270*(18): 2207–2212.

McGivern, D. O. 1993. The evolution to advanced nursing practice. *Nurses, nurse practitioners* (pp. 3–30), edited by Mezey, M. D., and McGivern, D. O. New York: Springer Publishing Company.

Meleis, A., and Trangenstein, P.1994. Facilitating transitions: Redefinition of the nursing mission. *Nursing Outlook, 42*(6): 255–259.

Mezey, M., and Lynaught, J. 1991. Teaching nursing home program: A lesson for quality. *Geriatric Nursing, 12*(2): 76–77.

Millis, J. S. 1966. *Report of the citizens' commission on graduate medical education.* The Graduate Education of Physicians. Chicago, IL: American Medical Association

Molde, S., and Diers, D. 1985. Nurse practitioner research: Selected literature review and research agenda. *Nursing Research, 34*(6): 362–367.

Moller, M. D. 1994, October. *The three R's program: Relapse, recovery, and rehabilitation.* Paper presented at the Eighth annual APNA conference, San Antonio, TX.

National Organization of Nurse Practitioner Faculties. 1994. Minutes of April board meeting. Washington, DC: Author.

———. 1995. *Advanced nursing practice: Nurse practitioner curriculum guidelines and program standards.* Washington, DC; Author.

Nichols, L. 1992. Estimating costs of undersizing advanced practice nurses. *Nursing Economics, 10*(5): 343–351.

Novinger, A. M. 1992. *College health: Vol. 3. Unique issues for nurse-directed college health centers* (pp. 558–565), edited by Patrick, K. Oakland, CA: Third Party Publishing Company.

Office of Technology Assessment (OTA). 1986, December. *Nurse practitioners, physician assistants, and certified midwives: A policy analysis.* Health technology case study #37, (20510–8025). Washington, DC: Author.

Pew Health Professions Commission. 1993, February. *Health professions education for the future: Schools in service to the nation.* University of California, San Francisco, CA: Center for the Health Professions.

————. 1994, April. *Nurse Practitioners. Doubling the graduates for the year 2000.* University of California, San Francisco, CA: Center for the Health Professions.

————. 1995 *Critical Challenges: Revitalizing the health professions for the twenty-first century.* University of California, San Francisco, CA: Center for the Health Professions.

Physician Payment Review Commission (PPRC). 1994. *Annual report to congress.* Washington, DC: Author.

Richards, R. 1994, June. *Community partnerships: Graduate medical and nursing education initiative.* Paper presented at the W. K. Kellogg Community Partnership Conference, Rosemont, IL.

Roback, G., Randolph, L., Seidman, B., and Pasko, T. 1994. *Physician characteristics and distribution in the US.* Chicago, IL: Survey and Data Resources, American Medical Association.

Robinson, C. A., Sepe, S. J., and Lin, K. F. Y. 1993. *The president's child immunization initiative—a summary of the problem and the response.* Public Health Reports, 108(4): 419–425.

Russell, L.B. 1992. *When is prevention better than cure? Charting nursing's future: Agenda for the 1990s* (pp. 60–69), edited by Aiken, L. H., and Fagin, C. M. Philadelphia: J. B. Lippincott.

Safreit, B. 1992. *Health care dollars and regulatory sense: The role of advanced practice nursing.* Yale Journal of Regulation, 9: 417–488.

Salmon, M.E. 1993. Public health nursing: The opportunity of a century. *American Journal of Public Health, 83:* 1674–1675.

Segal-Issacson, E. 1994. NP loses reimbursement of much of practice to bureaucratic muddle. *NP News, 2:* 1, 4.

Sekscenski, E., Sansom, S., Bazell, C., Salmon, M., and Mullan, F. 1994. State practice environments and supply of physician assistants, nurse practitioners, and certified nurse midwives. *New England Journal of Medicine, 131*(19): 1266–1271.

Schieber, G. J., Poullier, J. P., and Greenwald, L. M. 1994. Health system performance in OECD Countries, 1980–1992. *Health Affairs, 13*(2): 100–112.

Schroeder, S. A. 1992. Physician supply and the U.S. marketplace. *Health Affairs, 11*(1): 235–243.

Shugars, D. A., Vernon, T. M., Richardson, W. C., O'Neil, E. H., and Bader, J. D. 1991. Is health professions education part of the solution? *Health Affairs, 10*(4): 280–282.

Sox, H., and Woolf, S. 1993. Evidence-based guidelines from the U.S. Preventive Services Task Force. *Journal of the American Medical Association, 269*(20): 2678.

Starfield, B. 1992. *Primary care: Concept, evaluation, and policy.* New York, NY: Oxford University Press.

Stone, P. W. 1994. Nurse practitioners' research review: Quality of care. *Nurse Practitioner*, *19*(6): 17, 21, 27.

Sullivan, E., Fields, B., Kelly, J., and Whelan, E. M. 1993. Nursing centers: The new arena for advanced nursing practice. *Nurses, nurse practitioners* (pp. 251–264), edited by Mezey, M. D., and McGivern, D. O. New York: Springer Publishing Company.

Tengs, T. O., Adams, M. E.., Pliskin, J. S., Safran, D. G., Siegel, J. E., Weinstein, M. C., and Graham, J. D. 1994. *Five-hundred life-saving interventions and their cost-effectiveness*. Manuscript submitted for publication. Cambridge, MA: Harvard University.

Trella, R. S. 1993. A multidisciplinary approach to case management of frail, hospitalized older adults. *Journal of Nursing Administration*, *23*(2): 20–26.

U.S. Public Health Service (USPHS). 1990. *Healthy people 2000: National health promotion and disease prevention objectives*. Washington, DC: U.S. Government Printing Office.

———. 1994. Put prevention into practice: Implementing preventive care. *Journal of the American Academy of Nurse Practitioners*, *6*(6): 257–266.

U.S. Senate, 1990, August 3. *The health objectives 2000 act* (Report 101–417). Washington, DC: Author.

U.S. Senate Committee on Appropriations. 1994. *Department of labor, health and human services, and education and related agencies appropriation bill, 1995* (Senate Report 103-318, Calendar No. 527).

Vanderbilt, M. 1994, August. *Legislative report to the National Nurse Practitioner Coalition*. Washington, DC: American Nurses Association.

Wald, L. 1934. *Windows on Henry Street*. Boston: Little, Brown, and Co.

Wells, T.J. 1993. One hundred years of powerful women: A conversation with Loretta Ford. *Public Health Nursing*, *10*(2): 72–77.

Wilson, J. S., and Leasure, R. 1991. Cruel and unusual punishment: The health care of women in prison. *Nurse Practitioner*, *16*(2): 32–39.

World Health Organization. 1978, September. *Primary health care: Report of the international conference on primary health care*, Alma Ata, U.S.S.R. (Serial No. 1). Geneva: Author.

Zentner, J., Dellinger, C., Adkins, W., and Greene, J. 1995. Nurse practitioner provided primary care: Managing health care costs in the workplace. *American Association of Occupational Health Nurses Journal*, *43*(1):52–53.

DATE DUE

DEC 1 5 2000			
DEC 2 7 2000			
MAY 2 7 2003			
GAYLORD			PRINTED IN U.S.A.